*Dear Carol,*
*To one poet — me.*
*Portia the poet*

# Sungsook

초성숙

## Korean War Poems

*Portia Choi*

## by Portia S. Choi

cover illustration by Gita Lloyd

Book design and editing by Alexa Mergen.

Printed and bound by createspace.

Text face is Optima, designed by Hermann Zapf, released in 1958. The font was also chosen for names engraved on the Vietnam Veterans Memorial in Washington, D.C., and is used by the Asian Art Museum of San Francisco.

Copyright © Portia S. Choi, 2013

## For

Young Yong Choi, my father

In Soon Choi, my mother

Carol S. Choi-Stuart, my sister

Charles Davis Stokes, missionary

each Korean affected by the Korean War

each soldier who fought for freedom in the Korean War

# Contents

*Forward 7*

*Oaksun, My Doll 11*

*Heartbeats 13*

*Train-Bridge 14*

*Ball of Rice 15*

*Going on the Train 16*

*Stream Washing 17*

*Escape 18*

*Dialogue between Husband in America and Wife in Korea 20*

*Face Powder 22*

*Spring Treats 24*

*Beauty Iron, Seoul 25*

*Bouquet of Spring Promises* 27

*Three Post-War Games and One Rule* 29

*Tear* 30

*Face of a Child* 32

*One* 34

*Acknowledgements* 36

*The Poet* 37

# Forward

The Korean War lasted 37 months, from June 1950 to July 1953. There were almost one million deaths among the soldiers from the various countries that fought in the war. The "North Korean" side consisted of Democratic People's Republic of Korea, People's Republic of China, and the Soviet Union. The "South Korean" side consisted of Republic of Korea, Australia, Belgium, Canada, Colombia, Ethiopia, France, Greece, Luxembourg, Netherlands, New Zealand, Philippines, South Africa, Thailand, Turkey, the United Kingdom, and the United States. Other countries that supported the "South Korean" side were Denmark, Italy, Norway, India, Sweden with medical staff, and Japan with naval support and military services.

The war caused millions of casualties among civilian men, women and children, and several million people were made homeless. I, Sungsook, was among the homeless. I was two years old when the Korean War, also known as the Korean Conflict, broke out. I lived in Korea with my mother and an older sister, Sungjin. My father was already in the United States to study to be ordained as a Christian minister. He had been a minister in Korea, but needed additional education to be ordained in the United States. My mother figured he might not go study in America, a life-long dream of his, if he knew she was pregnant (with me in her womb). She kept me secret from Father until after he arrived in the U.S.

Communication between my parents was interrupted during the war. For many months, my father did not know whether his wife and two daughters, left behind in Korea, were alive. My mother contacted the American missionaries in Korea who were with the Board of Global Ministries of the Methodist Church. The missionaries contacted the U.S. Board and told them about our situation. When my father, in America, contacted the U.S. Board of Global Ministries, they were able to give him the news that his family was alive.

At age eight, I came to Los Angeles and was given a new name, Portia. My father wanted his daughters to have meaningful English names. My parents knew the Korean Methodist bishop in Los Angeles, and they discussed names with him and his wife. It was an honor to have the bishop involved in selecting new names for us. They all liked Shakespeare, especially the protagonist in "The Merchant of Venice," Portia.

I have remembered what my mother told me about the war. I also remember my experiences. As an adult, I met American veterans who served in the Korean War and they shared their stories with me. Many memories are collected in the poems.

Korea continues to be divided with an armistice, but no peace treaty. More than 59 years after the war's end, I do not know what happened to my relatives who remained in North Korea.

Portia S. Choi
Bakersfield, California
January 2013

**Oaksun, My Doll**

Oaksun, you are my love,
you make me smile
Oaksun, my dear Oaksun,
dressed in silk stripes of grass green, tomato red,
butterfly yellow, and sky blue.
Your slip sewn together of tattered, thrown-away clothes.

I find a torn piece of red balloon among pebbles and dirt near the chain fence.
I suck a circle into my mouth, out pops a rounded, shiny ball.
My teeth rub back and forth, squeaking the rubber.
For you, Oaksun, your balloon.

I am your mother, Oaksun.
I will protect and hide you from the soldiers.
I will look for you, so you cannot see the shattered arms.
I will cuddle you to sleep, so you cannot hear the cries.

I protect you.
You know Oaksun, I am frightened of the night.
I think that dying man may grab for you in the dark.
I will hide you.
Oaksun, no one will take you from me.

I feed you a kernel or two of rice. I find one stuck on your cheek.
Just a kernel dried from yesterday's dinner.
You are very lucky, Oaksun, having rice two days in a row.
You are very smart, too, saving one for tomorrow.
Yes, Oaksun, who knows when we will eat again?

The sun is out. There is clover among the grass, Oaksun.
See, I made a bracelet for you and a ring for me,
the white crescent flowers and the three leaves playing together.
I toss you up in the sky. You fall face-down in my palms.
I toss you again, you fall with your back down.
Fly higher and higher, Oaksun.

You are with me and I am with you.
I am your mother. Oaksun, my love, my doll.

## Heartbeats

Up and down
up and down
rocked on back of mama.
My arms grasp her,
my legs dangle
my bottom and back
tied to mama
with strips of cloth.

(Before, before
inside mama's water-warmth
her heartbeats muffled.)

Mama's arms support
my bottom, her heartbeats
through her blouse like
on slow walks from church,
rocked to sleep, home.

Shouts, awake,
rush, frenzy;
a grandma
falling down.

Mama's heartbeats.
I am on her back,
protected

in the sweat-blood rush
of refugees.

**Train-Bridge**

Click clack, click clack
clickety clack, clickety clack
dozing in the dark womb of war

inside train:
leaning on sister,
sweat smell, air heavy

under bridge:
leaning on mama,
urine stench, breeze stinging

cugh-cugh, uh-ug, ah-yah, uhm--inside train
uhm, ah-yah, cugh-cugh, uh-ug--under bridge

dozing in the dark womb of war

passing light, hut far away--inside train
birds chirping, light lifting--under bridge

stomach--grumble grumble grumble

Inside train--under bridge

train bridge, tra bri, click clak, trabri
trabritrabri trabritrabri trabritrabri trabritrabri

dozing in the dark womb of war.

**Ball of Rice**

My ball of rice: nice

warm, light and bright.

All darkness: faces, many places.

Darkness: bombs, red flashes, cries.

Where is mother?

Where is sister?

    Gone.

    Alone.

## Going on the Train

Remembering Myungja
in the field picking clover--
white flowers with pink tips and
green leaves with white strokes,
in her little hand, giving to me,
sweet--so sweet.

This little girl now
staring at me.
I had taken out my yam

munch on it, a little rice,
taken out from the cloth bundle.
Those eyes gaunt at me!

Oh--the food
I could give her--a little.
No!

She is not *my* girl--
I need this for me--to live--
to live and get to. . .
where?

She is staring
at me, she is crying.
No! this food is for me--to live.
Oh, but she looks like
Myungja,
my girl.
I buried her.

**Stream Washing**

A crisp sunny day;
    clear skies, yellow butterflies.

Clack clack clacking,
    mumbling and laughter.
Women at a stream's edge pounding away
    at trousers, shorts, skirts, blouses.
    Using their wooden paddles to beat out dirt, sweat;
    clean away fear, grief, anger, longing, fatigue.

Paddles in unison beating,
    water splashing faces,
    long skirts pulled up between legs,
    barefoot,
    squatted firmly in water.

The women hum the song of Spring Maiden
    who brought flowers and sweetness.
Then they gossip:
    *Oh, is that so?*
    *Can it be?*
    *Yes, she put her dead baby to her breast,*
        *carried it on her back.*
    *Oh, can it be!*

The children are shooed away to pick up pretty pebbles,
    or make clover-flower rings and bracelets,
    or watch the leaves drifting
    to their happy home.

**Escape**

My head nestled on mama's arm, and she told me
                                      about the war.

Mama whispered,
    "Your face, just to see your face again,
    kept me walking.
    I was being pushed
    up a hill with others, other Christians,
    wrists tied in a rope.
    All I could do was pray,
    and I remembered the verse in Romans:
    *In all things look to God.*
    And I witnessed to the soldier,
    that Jesus died for us, all of us, him too.
    Jesus had forgiven us of any wrong doing,
    just believe in Him and His goodness.
    The soldier told me
    to be quiet, such nonsense.
    I just kept praying then humming,
    humming sweet hymns:
    *Lord lead me onto higher grounds.*
    The soldier angered.
    He was at the tail end of the group.
    At the top of the hill,
    he told me to go down the hill quietly
    to run away fast.

> Some of the others, I heard, were
> beaten and killed.
> That soldier let me go--
> I am here with you."

I remember that time.
Mama showed up after a long while.
I remember her smile. tears,
how she moved so slowly.

## Dialogue between Husband in America and Wife in Korea

Dear wife, I am overjoyed to learn from the missionaries that you are alive, and also Sungjin and Sungsook. Before talking to the missionaries, I did not know where you were. The only news that I had about the war was from the newspaper and radio. I was so worried, I could not eat or study.

*My dear, you have always been able to study. You were a farmer's son and you studied so hard. Even in elementary school, you worked hard for the tuition. You wiped tables, swept floors, anything for tuition. You studied so hard, the missionaries recommended you to study for the ministry.*

We were so happy. I was an assistant minister and you were the Sunday school director. We were also blessed with Sungjin, our daughter. Then I had a chance to study in America. An answer to my prayers.

*Yes, dear, your dream to study in America. You had studied English into the night, hoping one day you would get to study, in America. We were getting prepared for you to leave.*

Dear wife, last month before I left Korea, you looked so tired in the mornings. You said it was because of all the preparation. I was so happy to go. I noticed that you would get up early and go outside, and return looking so exhausted. But I believed you.

*Yes, dear, how could I tell you I was pregnant. I wrote you after you were in America, that Sungsook was born. We had planned for me to join you in America, for me to study also. But how could I leave our young daughters, in Korea?*

Dear wife, when the war broke out, I was in such turmoil. I thought I was following God's calling. But was it just my pride? to study in America? When I did not know where you were, lost in the war. I prayed and went to the missionary board, and asked about you. I was overjoyed to learn that they had contact with you. Dear wife, God is faithful. One day, you will be in America. We will serve our Savior, together.

**Face Powder**

Mama slowly shuffled in,
>her arms around a big box and our helper lifting the other end.

Mama smiled excitedly, a smile that I did not often see.
>With scissors and a knife,
>>she slit open the flaps and brought out round powder boxes--
>>orange, gold and white cylinders wrapped in clear   paper,
>>so pretty and bright; and pictures of powder puffs of lightness.
>>"These will sell and for a good price, better than pencils,"
>mother whispered,
>>"The young single ones and even the grandmothers will want them."

I asked, "Ma-ma what are they for?"

Mama replied, "They are for the ladies to make them pretty."

I remembered at the refugee camp,
>a lady slowly taking out a compact, and
>>dab-dabbing her face;

putting powder on her nose, forehead, chin and
        cheek;
she studied her face turning side-to-side, and
        scrunched her mouth.
It made her face look lighter and chalky.

Mama said, "These will bring in the money.
    I remember the day I went to see that lady in the
            big house on the hill.
    People said, she has money and if you ask
            humbly--
    I went to see her, but the way she looked at me!
    I just couldn't ask, even though we were hungry.
    I prayed while walking back.
    That's when I thought of going to the
            missionaries
    to contact your father in America.
    I wrote him, and at first he sent me pencils.
    Then the ladies said, send for face powder,
            lipstick--
    anything to make us beautiful and feel
            luxurious--
    this is what your father sent."

Mama kept taking out more and more of the orange,
        gold, white powder boxes.
    At the bottom of the big box was candy--green,
        yellow and red;
    and a letter from Papa.

**Spring Treats**

In the hush of early spring,

      sun's brightness awakens tender sprigs beneath
          the melting snow.

        Squeals of other children entice
           me outside.  I speed into the
              marketplace.

A tan tube of billowing cloth undulates
    from pop-popping rice--

        Roasty aroma fills my nose.

      A man takes huge scissors, snips the candy brick
        lying on his cart.

    With red-puffy fingers, he picks up the candy,
      reaches to us crowded

        'round his cart.

      Ah-ah, yuh-yum. Sweetness melting

all around--

    taste safety.

## Beauty Iron, Seoul

She shoves curling iron rods into hot coals in the middle of the room. I sit nervously, squirming. I do not like those curlers. When the curling iron rods start to glow, she takes one out and waves it in the air a few times and wraps my hair round the rod with a wooden paddle. She puts the rod back into the coals, takes another out; over and over again. We are in Seoul. "So much to do," mother says. I see long streets, ladies and men in their thick blouses and trousers. The ladies' hair wrapped up in cloth; their hands reddened and rough. A few sell roasted chestnuts in newspaper cones. Mother changes sister and me into the smoothly ironed dresses, saying, "So pretty. The officers will look at you and think such pretty girls deserve their visas to America." At the government building, waiting and waiting and waiting. Mother hands forms to a man who never looks at us. He gives mother three cups. Mother hands the shallow cups to my older sister and me. She whispers, "Sungjin and Sungsook, go to the bathroom and give some stool. Put in the cup the stool that comes out last. The ladies in the line said the last ones do not have worms." After giving the cup to mother, there's more waiting and waiting. Then mother says, "Let's go."

On the train, mother brings out the newspaper cone and peels the cracked chestnuts. Eating the sweet kernels, the clickity clack of the wheels does not bother me. After our trip to Seoul, at home, on our street, I swirl my hair, showing my curls to the other girls.

## Bouquet of Spring Promises

Awakened from spring drowsiness,

toasty warm within quilts warmed by the *ondool* floor,
a floor heated by the ashes of coal and wood
pushed in from the kitchen hearth.

Mother chided us to dress,
and go into the hill to bring home
the tender herbs to make *namool*,
a salad mixed with sesame oil and vinegar.

Grimacing into cold dresses,
we gulped the warm, steaming rice
with pieces of salted black beans
and bites of radish *kim-chee*.

Slipping on our rubber shoes,
we ran through the front dirt yard,
scattered cackling chickens
and dodged bell-clanging goats.

Pushing open the massive wooden door, into the field,
we ran looking at two girls swinging higher and higher,
standing together on a wooden slat, heads thrust back,
upward into the sky of apple blossoms.

We rushed through gardens reeking with night soil,
filled with green onion and lettuce.

We balanced with outstretched arms,
on mounds dividing the rice paddies.

Up the hill, scampering zig-zag to outwit snakes,
we picked the stooped poppies, calling them grandmothers.
Finding the green sprigs, we pinched the tops,
or pulled the entire plant of leaves, roots and clinging dirt.

We rushed back to mother,
our hands full with bouquets of spring promises.

## Three Post-War Games and One Rule

1. Korean jacks: pebbles found in the dirt,
   our eyes stung by the dust of army jeeps.

2. Torn, thin rubber makes tiny balloons
   that squeak when squeezed on teeth.

3. We play chase in the park
   with limbs broken from trees
   as we watch legless soldiers piggyback
   on their friends.

   Rule: Never use branches as guns.

**Tear**

Thirty-eighth parallel,
      a line on a map, a simple line in a small country,
      a clean cut divides the spoils of war,
      North, South.

A not so simple dismembering of families:
      wife-husband, son-mother, brother-sister;
      a hand in the North, a leg in the South.

The heart pumping Kim, Shin, Pak, Kang, Chae blood
      drip, drip, dripping on the dirt,
      in the streams flowing over boulders
      in the Land of the Morning Calm.

Over a thousand days of Korean War;
      a woman screaming, her husband dragged away,
      her infant frozen and dead,
            no place to rest, no rice to eat.
      a little girl looking around,
      gunshots scattering birds.

I weep,
      for my country torn apart by a line.

Years and years pass,
      gathering now pieces of memory.

We exhume the dead, we exhume and release

uneasy spirits buried in the ever-present deathliness
of walking, walking, walking;
taking the threads of our memories, knowing
    that we were there together.
Now mending the tears in our hearts.
Mending the legs and arms severed and buried.

Remembering
    gentle swaying breeze of cosmos
    and leaves whispering sorrow
    in the Land of the Morning Calm.

**Face of a Child**

Within war an 18-year-old soldier squints at the shore
on Inchon.
Walking in waves he sees smoke-filled countryside.
Wanting to return to the troop ship but ordered
onward he forges onto the shore with the waves.

Marching for weeks the soldier nears a village outside
Wonju.
Between rice-thatched huts he struggles among
dismembered bodies smells the stench of burned flesh.
He tastes bile and sweat. He clenches his jaw ready
to blast the enemy.

Through tears he views the face of a child
peering between slats of a hut.
He pushes the door slowly with his rifle and sees
crouched in the dark corner children of all ages.

Soldier and fight mates find more orphaned
abandoned children. Gathering them up
they run together each soldier with a child
on his shoulder to a hillside cave near the railroad
tracks. The soldiers leave the children with water and
rice and instructions to be very quiet.

Taking branches and rocks they camouflage the hideaway entrance.
The soldier waves goodbye prays for safety smiles at the face of a little girl.
In days ahead as he fires his rifle he thinks of the children in the cave.

On a smoky night the soldiers return to the hill rushing to the cave and pushing aside scorched branches.
Moonlight falls on sleeping faces.
They pick up the children and lift them into American army trucks. As the soldier waves his ebony arm
at the departing truck he sees
a Korean girl about two-years-old.

On body-wrenching marches all the rest of
the days of the war
splashing through bloody rivulets
the soldier moves forward.
He saved children. That girl forever sees him.

**One**

Eddie, Jack, John, Neal, Richard.
5 boys from Bakersfield left home to fight
a conflict between democracy and communism
in the 3rd battalion, 29th infantry regiment, 24th division
and were ambushed at Hadong Pass, the southern tip of Korea.
313 killed that day including Eddie, Jack, John, and Richard.
100 captured, 24 MIA.

Neal was on the ground, bullets, bodies all around,
dust and tears blinding. *Why did my mother let me go?*
He combat-crawled under bodies, ran to a river, united
with 2 more American soldiers, ran
to a road where they hailed a military jeep.

*I fought the North Korean communists all the way*
*to the Yalu River, a few miles from the Manchurian border.*
*The Chinese kept coming and coming like a tidal wave.*
*I had an M-1 rifle, but could not get the clips*
*out of the cloth bandoleer fast enough.*
*Swung that rifle like a baseball bat, remembered hand-*
*to-hand combat techniques Turkish soldiers had taught*
*me. Back-and-forth around the 38th parallel we fought.*

Neal lives again in Bakersfield.
2 Purple Hearts and 1 Bronze Star.
Quiet days. Nights of memories.
3 flags in the yard:
United States of America          POW          KIA

# Acknowledgements

"Tear" was previously published in *KoreAm Journal*.

"Oak-Sun, My Doll" was previously published in *Dolphins and Tin Cans*, and in the Writers of Kern anthology.

# The Poet

Portia S. Choi is a public health and preventative medicine physician. Previously a resident of Los Angeles, she enjoys a quieter life in Bakersfield with other community poets, and her husband and two sons. She helps organize the city's annual celebration of National Poetry Month, listens to music and grows flowers.

Contact Portia at ssportia@aol.com

Made in the USA
Lexington, KY
04 June 2018